Points of
VIEW

·N·O·R·T·H·E·R·N·
·I·R·E·L·A·N·D·

Sean O'Neill

Wayland

Points of View

Abortion
Advertising
Alcohol
Animal Rights
Censorship
Crime and Punishment
Divorce
Drugs

Medical Ethics
Northern Ireland
Nuclear Weapons
Pollution
Racism
Sex and Sexuality
Smoking
Terrorism

Acknowledgements

The publishers have attempted to contact all copyright holders of the quotations in this book, and apologize if there have been any oversights.

The publishers gratefully acknowledge permission from the following to reproduce copyright material: Bloomsbury Publishing Limited, for extracts from *Lies of Silence* by Brian Moore, 1990; Chatto & Windus, for an extract from *Ireland: Why Britain Must Get Out* by Paul Foot, 1989; Child Poverty Action Group, for an extract from *On the Edge: a study of poverty and long term unemployment in Northern Ireland* by Eileen Evason, 1985; Corgi, for an extract from *The Provisional IRA* by Patrick Bishop and Eamonn Mallie, 1988; Andre Deutsch, for extracts from *The Crack: A Belfast Year*, by Sally Belfrage, 1987; Faber & Faber for an extract from the poem 'Digging' by Seamus Heaney, in *New Selected Poems*, 1990; Fontana, for an extract from *The IRA* by Tim Pat Coogan, 1987; Gill and Macmillan, for: 1) extracts from *A History of Northern Ireland* by Patrick Buckland, 1981; 2) extracts from *Northern Ireland: the International Perspective* by Adrian Guelke, 1988; the *Guardian*, for: 1) an extract from 'Another Country' by Tim Marsh, 22 August 1990; 2) an extract from 'Fast Talkers and Fenians' by Peter Lennon, 17 July 1990; 3) extracts from a week of special features by Polly Toynbee, Michael Billington, 18-23 February 1980; Harrap, for an extract from *Stalker* by John Stalker, 1988; Hurst & Co, for: 1) an extract from *Loyal to King Billy: A Portrait of the Ulster Protestants* by Robert G Crawford, 1987; 2) an extract from *Under Siege* by Arthur Aughey, 1989; Hutchinson Radius, for extracts from *Unfinished Business* by Liam de Paor, 1990; Mercier Press, for an extract from *A Pathway to Peace* by Gerry Adams, 1988; Methuen, for an extract from *The RUC: A Force Under Fire* by Chris Ryder, 1989; O'Brien Press, for extracts from *Phrases make History Here* by Conor O'Clery, 1986; Penguin, for extracts from *Ireland: A Positive Proposal* by Kevin Boyle and Tom Hadden, 1985; Poolbeg, for an extract from *Paisley* by Ed Moloney and Andy Pollak, 1986; Sidgwick and Jackson, for an extract from *Northern Ireland Soldiers Talking* by Max Arthur, 1987; *The Times*, for an extract from an article by Charles Townshend, 9 August 1989; Weidenfeld & Nicholson, for an extract from *All Of Us There* by Polly Devlin, 1983; Zed Books, for an extract from *The Longest War* by Kevin J Kelly, 1988.

Front cover: *A street in Belfast.*

Editor: William Wharfe
Researcher: Sarah Boothby
Designer: David Armitage

First published in 1991 by
Wayland (Publishers) Limited
61 Western Road, Hove
East Sussex BN3 1JD, England

British Library Cataloguing in Publication Data
O'Neill, Sean
    Northern Ireland. — (Points of view)
    I. Title. II. Series
    941.60824

ISBN 1-85210-653-0

Phototypeset by Direct Image Photosetting Ltd,
Hove, East Sussex, England
Printed in Italy by G. Canale & C.S.p.A, Turin
Bound in France by A.G.M.

Contents

Northern Ireland: a brief history

On the morning of Easter Sunday 1916, when Europe was in the grip of the First World War and the whole of Ireland was governed by Britain, a small group of about 100 armed men stormed and occupied the General Post Office building in the centre of Dublin. Two of the group's leaders, James Connolly and Padraig Pearse, appeared on the steps of the building. Pearse read aloud, to the bewilderment of passers-by:

> We declare the right of the people of Ireland to the ownership of Ireland . . . The long usurpation of that right by a foreign people and government has not extinguished that right, nor can it ever be extinguished except by the destruction of the Irish people. In every generation the Irish people have asserted their right to national freedom and sovereignty; six times during the past 300 years they have asserted it in arms. Standing on that fundamental right and again asserting it in arms in the face of the world, we hereby proclaim the Irish Republic as a Sovereign Independent State . . . (Quoted in *The Longest War,* Kevin J Kelley.)

Members of the Citizen's Army, created by James Connolly, which took part in the 1916 Easter Rising, parading outside Liberty Hall in Dublin.

Many of the captured rebels of 1916 were taken at first to Richmond Barracks in Dublin, where their families were allowed to visit them three times a week. The leaders of the rebellion were held under tighter security at Kilmainham gaol before they were executed.

A week of fierce fighting followed on the streets of Dublin between the rebels and the British Army. The rebels were defeated, just as other armed revolts against British rule had been in the past. Crowds in the city jeered at and spat on the rebels as they were arrested and led away. But the mood of the people changed suddenly when the British began to execute the rebel leaders by firing squad. James Connolly was shot while strapped to a chair, still suffering wounds inflicted in the fighting. Their deaths won the sympathy of the majority of the Irish people for their cause.

The Irish writer George Bernard Shaw wrote, in a letter to a London newspaper:

> My own view is that the men who were shot in cold blood, after their capture or surrender, were prisoners of war, and that it was therefore entirely incorrect to slaughter them . . . It is absolutely impossible to slaughter a man in this position without making him a martyr and a hero. (Quoted in *Phrases Make History Here,* Conor O'Clery.)

Two years later, at a general election for the parliament in London, Sinn Fein (meaning 'Ourselves Alone'), a party which supported the rebels, won 73 of the 105 seats in Ireland. Its new Members of Parliament (MPs) refused to go to London, and set up their own parliament, called the Dail, in Dublin.

On the same day the Dail opened in 1919, the Irish Republican Army (IRA), a guerilla force descended from the 1916 rebels, carried out its first military operation against British forces and started the Irish War of Independence.

The Civil War 1922-23 produced bitter fighting between people who had fought together against the British. The war began in Dublin when forces of the newly formed Free State Army shelled positions held by their former IRA comrades, who wanted to fight on for an all-Ireland republic.

In 1920, while the war still raged, the British parliament at Westminster passed laws partitioning Ireland into two separate states. One, comprising the island's six north-eastern counties was called Northern Ireland and was to remain part of Britain. The other, made up of Ireland's remaining twenty-six counties, was to be named the Irish Free State.

The War of Independence ended in July 1921 when talks were held in London between a delegation of IRA leaders, headed by Michael Collins, and the British government. A treaty giving the southern twenty-six counties of Ireland limited independence was signed to stop the fighting. But hardline forces in the IRA, who wanted a single, independent Ireland, objected to the treaty. They fought and lost the bitter Civil War (1922-23) against their old allies who were prepared to accept the treaty. In 1948 the Free State cut all ties to the English throne and declared itself the Republic of Ireland.

The new state of Northern Ireland was made up of the six counties of Ireland where a majority of the people wanted to remain a part of Britain. They were mainly Protestants and supported the Unionist Party, so called because of its support for the Act of Union of 1800 which had formally tied Britain and Ireland together. Northern Ireland had its own parliament and government (between 1921 and 1972 the Unionist Party formed that government), but also elected MPs to the British parliament in London.

Northern Ireland's minority Catholic population was called nationalist because it largely favoured a united Ireland. Because of this it was regarded as disloyal by the Unionist government. James Craig, the Prime Minister of Northern Ireland, speaking in a debate about employment of 'disloyalists' in the Belfast parliament, said on 24 April 1934:

> All I boast of is that we are a Protestant Parliament and a Protestant State. (Quoted in *Phrases Make History Here*, Conor O'Clery.)

The IRA has carried out violent campaigns against the Northern Ireland Government in every decade of its existence. But in the late 1960s the IRA was virtually non-existent. A new, 'civil rights', movement emerged amongst the Catholic community. The civil rights campaigners concentrated on the issue of discrimination. Many Catholics felt that the Protestant-run Northern Ireland government discriminated against Catholics in the housing, employment and education it provided. The civil rights movement demanded equal rights for everyone in Northern Ireland and called for the establishment of fair elections in the province. One of the movement's slogans was 'British Rights for British Citizens'. The moderate Prime Minister, Terence O'Neill, tried to make reforms, but was largely prevented by unionist extremists who did not want any

These civil rights campaigners marching through Lurgan, County Armagh, in 1969 were demanding equal rights within Northern Ireland. They were not conducting a campaign for a united Ireland.

The Bogside area of Derry/Londonderry was the scene for some of the fiercest rioting at the beginning of the 'Troubles.' Rioting here led to the decision by the British government to send its troops to Northern Ireland in 1969. Here in 1972 rioters confront those troops shortly after Bloody Sunday, when British paratroopers killed 14 people on a civil rights march.

Chronology of events 1916–72:

1916	Easter Rising defeated in Dublin
1918	Sinn Fein win elections
1919	IRA begins war of independence
1920	Britain decides to partition Ireland
1921	Northern Ireland parliament opens
1922	Treaty ending independence war passed, but civil war begins in Southern Ireland
1948	Irish Free State declares itself a republic
1968	Civil rights marches begin in Northern Ireland
1969	British Army sent in to Northern Ireland
1972	Direct rule imposed on Northern Ireland from Britain

concessions to be made to the civil rights campaigners.

Unionist extremists attacked civil rights marches, often with the tacit co-operation of the predominantly Protestant police force and its back-up force, the notorious B Specials. In August 1969, following a fierce weekend of rioting in Derry/ Londonderry, when Catholics in the Bogside area were virtually besieged by the police and by violent Protestant gangs, the British government in London decided to send in its troops to keep law and order.

At first the troops were welcomed. Catholics saw them as protectors. Protestants thought they would put an end to the civil rights movement. After a year, with violence still continuing, the Catholics had lost faith in the Army and many turned towards the re-emerging IRA as their protector. The IRA argued that the Northern Ireland state would never end discrimination against the Catholic minority and that a united Ireland, free from Britain, was the best solution. In 1972 the British government decided that the government in Northern Ireland was no longer able to control the situation that was developing. It closed the parliament in Belfast and established a system of direct rule of Northern Ireland from London. That system is still in force.

Who governs Northern Ireland?

● The partition

> The boundary, which now separates Northern Ireland from
> the Republic, was first established by the Government of
> Ireland Act in 1920 and came into effect in British law in
> 1921 . . . The Act partitioned Ireland unevenly, separating
> 6,000 square miles [c. 15,500 km²] from 27,000 square miles
> [c. 69,900 km²] and dividing off one-and-a-half million people
> (of whom at that time 66 per cent were Protestants and 34
> per cent Catholics) from three million (of whom about 10 per
> cent were Protestants and about 90 per cent Catholics).
> (*Unfinished Business*, Liam de Paor.)

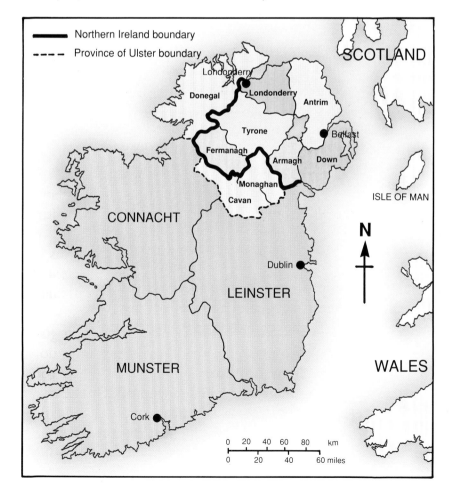

The Government of Ireland Act of 1920 separated six counties out of the nine counties of the ancient province of Ulster from the rest of Ireland. The counties of Donegal, Cavan and Monaghan, which had formerly been part of Ulster, became part of the Irish Free State, along with the provinces of Connacht, Leinster and Munster.

Residents of a Belfast street during the annual Orange Order marching season. The banners display anti-Catholic slogans such as: 'Ulster Won't to Popery Submit' and 'Home Rule is Rome Rule.'

Flags

Three flags are regularly flown in Northern Ireland. The unionists display the Union flag (flag of the United Kingdom) and the Ulster flag (a red cross on a white background with the mythical symbol of the Red Hand in the centre). Nationalists fly the Irish tricolour, the green white and orange flag of the Irish Republic which was originally meant to symbolize peace between the two communities in Ireland (green representing the Catholics, orange the Protestants).

The partition of Ireland was an attempt to solve what appeared to be an insoluble problem. The issue of Home Rule for Ireland had dominated British and Irish politics in the years before the First World War. In 1912 it had been accepted by the British parliament. But it was opposed strongly by the majority of the population in the north-east of the country which favoured keeping the link with Britain. They had the support of the British Conservative Party, then in opposition. In March 1917, speaking in the House of Commons, the Liberal Prime Minister David Lloyd George outlined his view of the problem:

> In the north-eastern portion of Ireland you have a population as hostile to Irish rule as the rest of Ireland is to British rule, yea, and as ready to rebel against it as the rest of Ireland is against British rule — as alien in blood, in religious faith, in traditions, in outlook — as alien from the rest of Ireland in this respect as the inhabitants of Fife or Aberdeen. (Quoted in *Phrases Make History Here,* Conor O'Clery.)

After the 1916 rebellion, the unionists were persuaded that the only way to avoid Home Rule was to accept their own parliament in the six north-eastern counties. In 1921 the counties of Antrim (where the capital Belfast is situated), Armagh, Derry/Londonderry, Down, Fermanagh and Tyrone were separated from the rest of Ireland because they guaranteed the new state a Protestant majority which would be certain to elect a government to support the continued link with Britain.

Northern Ireland is often incorrectly called 'Ulster'. Ulster is the name of one of the four ancient provinces of Ireland and actually contains nine counties — the six named above plus the counties of Cavan, Donegal and Monaghan.

In 1988 Northern Ireland's population was just under 1.6 million. Protestants account for about 60 per cent of the population, with Catholics making up the remaining 40 per cent.

● **Government from London**

Northern Ireland is part of the United Kingdom of Great Britain and Northern Ireland. Its people are citizens of the UK and abide by laws passed in the UK parliament at Westminster. Some legislation is passed which applies specifically to Northern Ireland. On 10 November 1981 the then British Prime Minister

Stormont Castle near Belfast, where the Northern Ireland parliament met from 1921 to 1972.

What's in a name?

Northern Ireland's second city is Derry or Londonderry. Nationalists call the city Derry, a name derived from the Irish language version Doire. Unionists prefer Londonderry, a name given in tribute to the role played by City of London companies in the city's development. The city council is called Derry, but the official title of the city is Londonderry. In the same way, the county in which the city is situated is known as Derry to nationalists and Londonderry to unionists.

Margaret Thatcher (MP for Finchley in North London) answered a question in the House of Commons with the reply:

> Northern Ireland is part of the United Kingdom – as much as my constituency is. (Quoted in *Phrases Make History Here*, Conor O'Clery.)

Since 1972, when the parliament in Belfast was suspended, the British government has appointed a minister, known as the Secretary of State for Northern Ireland, to be responsible for policy in the region. The system is known as 'direct rule', and the minister is responsible for policies on security, finance, health, agriculture, social affairs and other major areas. The Secretary of State has always been an MP elected to represent a British constituency and never one of the MPs elected to Westminster by the voters of the seventeen parliamentary constituencies in Northern Ireland.

Dr Garret FitzGerald, Taoiseach (Prime Minister) of the Irish Republic, and Margaret Thatcher, Prime Minister of the UK, display copies of the Anglo-Irish Agreement signed on 15 November, 1985. Also pictured is Tom King, then Secretary of State for Northern Ireland. The Agreement set down procedures for consultation between the two governments over Northern Ireland issues. The people of Northern Ireland were not consulted about it.

● Dublin's claim

The people of Northern Ireland can also be citizens of the Irish Republic. Under its 1937 constitution the Republic lays claim to Northern Ireland.

> Article 2. The national territory consists of the whole island of Ireland, its islands and the territorial seas.
> Article 3. Pending the reintegration of the national territory, and without prejudice to the right of the Parliament and Government established by this Constitution to exercise over the whole of that territory, the laws enacted by that Parliament shall have the like area and extent of application as the laws of Saorstat Eireann [the Irish Free State] . . .

The constitution thus claims that the government of the Republic of Ireland has the right to govern the whole island of Ireland and states the Republic's desire to reunite Ireland.

● The Anglo-Irish Agreement

The Republic of Ireland has never attempted to enforce its constitutional claim to the right to govern Northern Ireland. There have been political disputes with the government in London, but the two countries have not gone to war over the issue. Indeed in 1985, the British and Irish governments signed the Anglo-Irish Agreement, representing a new era in the government of Northern Ireland. It established a conference at which views of ministers from the UK and from the Irish Republic could be exchanged concerning the government of Northern Ireland.

A new president

In 1990 the Irish Republic elected its first woman president, Mary Robinson. Although the post of president is largely honorary (the government is headed by the Taoiseach or Prime Minister) her election is seen as a sign of a new liberalism in Ireland, especially on matters such as divorce and contraception. Mrs Robinson has also encouraged talks with the unionists of Northern Ireland.

Do you think Northern Ireland is British or Irish?

> The two Governments . . . affirm that any change in the status of Northern Ireland would only come about with the consent of a majority of the people of Northern Ireland . . . The United Kingdom Government accept that the Irish Government will put forward views and proposals on matters relating to Northern Ireland . . . In the interests of promoting peace and stability, determined efforts shall be made through the conference to resolve any differences. (Articles 1 and 2 of the Anglo-Irish Agreement, signed 15 November 1985.)

The Irish government seemed to say that Ireland would only be reunited and governed from Dublin when the people of Northern Ireland agreed to unity. The British government appeared to be saying in the Agreement that it would allow the Irish government to influence how Northern Ireland, a part of the UK, would be governed.

The Agreement provoked anger from unionists in Northern Ireland. They argued that they had not been consulted about a decision on how they would be governed. They said the Agreement was treacherous. It also angered Irish Republicans who believed the Irish government had renounced its claim on the six Northern counties, and made a united Ireland more unlikely. But it was widely welcomed in the British parliament, by moderate politicians in both Northern Ireland and the Republic, by church leaders and by the international community. The then President of the USA, Ronald Reagan, commented on the Agreement:

> We applaud its promise of peace and a new dawn for the troubled communities of Northern Ireland. (Speech in Washington, USA, 15 November, 1985.)

Loyalists have opposed any moves which appeared to weaken their domination of Northern Ireland. In 1971 they marched on the government buildings at Stormont to protest that the Unionist government was making too many pro-Catholic reforms. They wanted the Prime Minister James Chichester Clark replaced by the anti-reform William Craig.

13

What are the dividing lines?

● The power struggle

Northern Ireland's 'Troubles' are often portrayed as a religious war between two tribes, with the British Army trying to keep them apart. But the religious terms Protestant and Catholic are often used to simplify and confuse longstanding conflicts over power, economics, land and the border. Many commentators have observed that the two communities are not divided about churchgoing, but about whether they see themselves as Irish or British.

The Protestants of Northern Ireland originate from English and Scottish settlers who were given land in Ireland, predominantly in Ulster, by King James I (King of England, Wales, Scotland and Ireland) in 1608. In an attempt to make Ireland easier to govern the English drove the native Catholic people off their land and gave the best land to the settlers. The event was known as the Plantation of Ulster. In 1641 the native Irish rebelled against the settlers, killing many of them. But by the end of the century the Protestant ascendancy in Ireland, and in particular Ulster, had been established.

A mural on a Belfast street celebrates King William III, the Prince of Orange, who in 1690 came to Ireland and defeated the Catholic King James II at the Battle of the Boyne, ensuring that only a Protestant could sit on the English throne. Political murals are a common feature in both Catholic and Protestant areas of Belfast.

A Catholic family with their few possessions outside the home they have just been evicted from. This scene, from County Fermanagh in the 1890s, was typical of the way Catholics were driven off the best farming land.

The historian Patrick Buckland summed up the origins of the Protestant – Catholic conflict and the emergence, with British help, of Protestant domination in Ireland:

> The influx of settlers from England and Scotland had hardly been welcomed by the ... Catholic host community, deprived of its traditions and often its land – certainly its best land. Whereas the ... Irish resented and remembered the foreign occupation, Ulster Protestants long recalled with horror attempts to massacre and expel them. It was not until the end of the seventeenth century that doubts about the future of Protestants in Ireland were resolved, as Irish Protestants sided with the Protestant William of Orange in his successful attempt to wrest the English throne from the Catholic James II [in 1690] ... Thenceforth, the Protestant minority ruled Ireland. The Protestants in the North dominated Ulster.
> (*A History of Northern Ireland,* Patrick Buckland.)

The eighteenth century began with the native Irish subdued under laws which outlawed the Catholic religion. Many of the laws were removed by the mid-1700s, but it was not until 1829, nearly three decades after the Act of Union (passed in 1800), that any Catholics were able to vote. From then on the majority of Irish politicians were dedicated to achieving some form of independence for Ireland. They talked of 'Home Rule for Ireland'. Protestant politicians elected from Ulster wanted to maintain the Act of Union and its guarantees of their dominance in Ireland. The two sides fought long political battles over three Home Rule bills in 1886, 1893 and 1912.

Members of the Orange Order, wearing their traditional sashes, marching with a band through Portadown, County Armagh. Their banner displays 'King Billy' (William III) on his white charger.

Following the 1916 rebellion and the War of Independence (see chapter one) the Northern Ireland state remained as a stronghold of unionist political and economic power. At that time the Belfast shipyards and textile industries were internationally powerful. Protestants have been encouraged to believe in their numerical, economic and social superiority. Protestant dominance has been celebrated every summer through parades by the Orange Order. The Order's big day is 12 July, when Protestant men and youths from all over Northern Ireland and abroad march to commemorate William of Orange's victory in Ireland over the Catholic King James II at the Battle of the Boyne in 1690. The battle ensured that only a Protestant could sit on the English throne.

● Class and creed

Religion still plays a large part in Northern Ireland politics. Often it obscures other social and economic divisions which also influence the politics of the region. In 1932 Protestant and Catholic people from Belfast's working-class districts united in demonstrations against high unemployment and low relief payments to the poor. Tommy Geehan, a left-wing leader of the Belfast demonstrations hailed the events:

> For many years the workers of Belfast had been divided by artificial barriers of religion and politics but the past two months had witnessed a wonderful spectacle because the workers were now united on a common platform demanding the right to live. (*Belfast Newsletter*, 11 October 1932.)

> **Catholic and Protestant**
> The Catholic and Protestant Churches are both Christian but worship in different ways and stress different aspects of Christianity. However, the terms Catholic and Protestant distinguish more than religious differences in Northern Ireland. The term Catholic is used to refer to the people who are the 'native' Irish, dispossessed of land and persecuted for their religion by the British. The term Protestant is used in relation to people whose ancestors came from Britain to occupy land taken away from the native Irish. The tensions between the groups are more to do with those historical conflicts than the religious differences that exist today.

The demonstrations were beaten down by police and became violent. The government of Northern Ireland, which largely represented the leaders of industry, did not want ideas of class politics to spread. It told people the demonstrations were the work of Republicans and raised the spectre of the IRA to win back the support of Protestants. John Campbell of the Northern Ireland Labour Party attacked the Unionist government of the time under the Northern Ireland Prime Minister Lord Craigavon:

> Lord Craigavon's solution was to divide the workers into different religious camps and it was noteworthy that although the recent trouble was spread all over the city, only in a Roman Catholic area did the police use their guns. (*Belfast Newsletter*, 17 October 1932.)

The tactics served to remind Protestants of their superiority in Northern Ireland and to frighten them into believing that Catholic demonstrators wanted to overthrow the Protestant state. In his novel *Lies of Silence*, award-winning Irish writer Brian Moore complains that the authorities in Northern Ireland emphasize the differences between Catholics and Protestants, rather than what they have in common.

> Dillon felt anger rise within him, anger at the lies which had made this, his . . . birthplace, sick with a terminal illness of bigotry and injustice, lies told over the years to poor Protestant working people about the Catholics, lies told to poor Catholic working people about the Protestants, lies from parliaments and pulpits, lies at rallies and funeral orations, and, above all, the lies of silence from those in Westminster who did not want to face the injustices of Ulster's status quo. (*Lies of Silence*, Brian Moore.)

The dividing lines between Catholics and Protestants, nationalists and unionists are not so clear, says the Irish historian Liam de Paor.

> There is a strong negative element in both nationalism and loyalism in the North. Nationalists resent, not so much British rule as Unionist rule with British backing. They look to the South with somewhat mixed feelings. Loyalists are not so much attached to the political connection to Britain . . . as determined not to be brought under Dublin rule. (*Unfinished Business*, Liam de Paor.)

Pope John Paul II arrives in Ireland in 1979. His open-air masses attracted hundreds of thousands of people. He did not visit Northern Ireland, but at a mass at Drogheda, just south of the border, he pleaded for an end to violence.

Brand names
Not only are 'Catholic' and 'Protestant' inadequate explanations for political divisions in Northern Ireland, so are unionist and nationalist. The more extreme factions on both sides are generally referred to by other names. Hardline unionists, including those who adopt violence, are generally called Loyalists. Hardline nationalists, including the IRA, prefer to be known as Republicans.

Some unionists want integration of Northern Ireland into the rest of the UK, others want a separate unionist government returned to Northern Ireland. Some nationalists are prepared to discuss a coalition government with unionists in Northern Ireland. There are different visions of what a united Ireland would be like (see final chapter).

Much Protestant unionist political strength arises from the bonding together of different groups through a common fear.

> Ulster Protestants . . . are by no means a homogenous group. Throughout their history they have been divided in almost all the ways in which a society can be divided into classes, groups and opinions . . . But since quite early in the nineteenth century, Protestant Ulster has been drawn together, and frequently forced together, by a single issue which more and more assumed the character of a threat: the possibility of a Dublin, Catholic government of all Ireland. (*Unfinished Business*, Liam de Paor.)

The political career of Ian Paisley clearly links religion and politics in Northern Ireland. He is head of the Free Presbyterian Church and leader of the Democratic Unionist Party. Ian Paisley's politics are dominated by the belief that a Protestant Northern Ireland must never be swallowed up by a Catholic all-Ireland state.

Political parties

The four largest political parties in Northern Ireland are divided on class lines as well as by nationalist and unionist differences. The Ulster Unionist Party attracts mainly Protestant middle-class support. The Democratic Unionist Party appeals to the Protestant working class. The nationalist Social Democratic and Labour Party draws support from the Catholic middle and working classes. Sinn Fein, the political wing of the IRA, has its support firmly rooted in the Catholic working class. Two other parties present a non-sectarian image. The Alliance Party attracts middle-class support across the divide, while the Workers' Party attempts to win working-class support for its left-wing policies.

Opposite *Loyalist grafitti in Belfast, including slogans supporting the paramilitary Ulster Volunteer Force.*

Right *Prostestant leader Ian Paisley leads a protest against the Anglo-Irish Agreement.*

In 1958 Paisley wrote:

> The dark sinister shadow of our neighbouring Roman Catholic state, where religious liberty is slowly but surely being taken away, lies across our province . . . Not only have we this enemy without but we have a strong fifth column of sympathizers and compromisers within. The only effective answer to encroaching Romanism [Catholicism] is a revived and revitalized Protestantism. (Quoted in *Paisley*, Ed Moloney and Andy Pollak.)

Supporters of Paisley's party have a strong influence in Northern Ireland. They have succeeded in closing parks, swimming pools and other recreational facilities on Sundays because that is the Christian sabbath. They have protested against a gay rights conference in Belfast under the banner 'Save Ulster from Sodomy'. They have successfully opposed the extension of British abortion and divorce laws to Northern Ireland. Abortion is illegal in Northern Ireland (as it is in the Republic), and married couples there who wish to divorce must first go through a two-year trial separation – which is not required in the rest of the UK.

The Catholic Church is also active in the political and social life of Northern Ireland. It demands that its adherents send their children to Catholic schools. The Church has been one of the strongest opponents of moves towards educating Catholic and Protestant children in the same schools. Around 99 per cent of Catholic and Protestant children attend separate schools. Often they live in different areas and never meet.

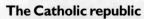

The Catholic republic

The Catholic Church remains a very influential force in Southern Ireland. Since partition, the number of Protestants living in the south has fallen by half; today only 3 per cent of the population of the Republic is Protestant. The Catholic Church was very active in recent successful campaigns to include bans on abortion and divorce in the constitution.

Catholics attending Sunday Mass at a crowded church in the Ardoyne area of Belfast.

1 Do you think religion is the main issue in Northern Ireland?

2 What do you think unionists and nationalists want?

3 Are Northern Ireland politics different from those in your own country? In what way?

4 Do you think the people of Northern Ireland have the right to segregated education, or should all schools in the region be obliged to take both Catholic and Protestant pupils?

5 Are you religious? Does the religion of other people affect the way you think about them? Why? How would do you feel about another person's opinion of you being influenced by your religious beliefs (or lack of them)?

> A recent initiative to unite the two teacher training colleges, Catholic and Protestant, had failed largely through Catholic Church opposition. Pressure had been exerted on children to get parents' signatures opposing it; petitions were passed down pews at Mass. A first step toward integrating education in general, the college merger was 'portrayed by the Church as an act against Catholics, another attack on the Catholic religion'. (*The Crack: A Belfast Year,* Sally Belfrage.)

Protestants and Catholics are still separated and segregated in Northern Ireland. In Belfast a tall wall divides Catholic streets from Protestant streets – it is known as the Peace Line. And there is evidence that Catholics still experience discrimination: Catholic males are two-and-a-half times more likely to be unemployed than Protestants. Commenting on the problem of sectarian gang-fighting in his town, Michael McLoughlin, former chairman of Dungannon council in County Tyrone, said:

> These young people have learned all their politics, their attitudes to society, growing up in segregated schools, segregated housing estates and segregated youth clubs. They never meet, they've never met. I don't expect them to be any different to what they are. There are entrenched attitudes on both sides, I don't expect that to change overnight. (Interview with author, June 1990.)

Keeping the peace?

Northern Ireland is policed by a large force of armed police and soldiers – collectively known as the security forces. Such extensive security forces have become the centre of a controversy over whether they do more harm than good – they are expensive to run and often intrude on the life of ordinary people in the region. However, as long as paramilitary groups continue to carry out terrorist attacks, governments in Britain have remained reluctant to reduce the security forces.

● The British Army in Northern Ireland

Since the British government decided to send in troops to Northern Ireland in 1969, there has been a continuing debate as to whether they should be withdrawn. In recent years, opinion polls have repeatedly shown a majority of British people in favour of withdrawal; a 1987 poll in the *Daily Express* showed that 61 per cent of British people favoured withdrawal. This feeling has partly been caused by the cost of keeping the Army in Northern Ireland. By the end of 1989 Britain was spending £5 billion per year on governing Northern Ireland.

> **The cost of peace-keeping**
>
> Between 1969 and 1985, the British Government paid out more than £1 billion in compensation for damage to property as a result of the violence in Northern Ireland. If violence had occurred to the same extent in Britain itself, the corresponding compensation figure would have been £40 billion (Note: 1 billion = 1,000,000,000).

When British troops arrived in Northern Ireland in 1969 they were welcomed with tea and biscuits by Catholic families whose streets and homes had been under attack. The Catholics thought the troops were there to protect them.

Some people in high places think it is too much. Even back in 1982, Lord Gowrie, then a British government junior minister for Northern Ireland, said in a speech to the Irish Club in London:

> Northern Ireland is extremely expensive on the British taxpayer . . . if the people of Northern Ireland wished to join with the South of Ireland, no British Government would resist it for twenty minutes. (Quoted in *Phrases Make History Here,* Conor O'Clery.)

The British Army is often described as a peacekeeping force in Northern Ireland. It was sent there in 1969 at a time of violent strife between the two communities. The Army suffered 432 deaths between 1969 and 1989. If the Army was to pull out, many people feel there would be a massive increase in violence.

> People in Britain are always saying pull the troops out. To me that's inconceivable. I don't think the general public understand what it would mean, I don't think they understand the precedent it would set. I can't even imagine why anyone would think that nothing would happen. It would be a civil war, it would be appalling, even worse than it is now.
> (A Sergeant Major in the Royal Green Jackets, quoted in *Northern Ireland Soldiers Talking,* Max Arthur.)

British troops confront crowds on 30 January 1972 in Derry/Londonderry, the day known as Bloody Sunday.

In 1978 Margaret Thatcher MP, then leader of the parliamentary opposition in Britain, answered calls for British withdrawal by saying:

> If you wash your hands of Northern Ireland, you wash them in blood. (Quoted in *Phrases Make History Here,* Conor O'Clery.)

But others argue that the Army has become part of the problem. In one infamous incident on 30 January 1972 the British Parachute Regiment opened fire on a civil rights march in Derry/Londonderry. Catholic priests in the city, some of whom had been present at the march, condemned the soldiers in forthright terms:

> We accuse the Commander of Land Forces [the British Army] of being an accessory after the fact. We accuse the soldiers of firing indiscriminately into a fleeing crowd, of gloating over casualties . . . these men are trained criminals. They differ from terrorists only in the veneer of respectability that a uniform gives them.

The day became known as Bloody Sunday. The Coroner condemned the killings as 'sheer unadulterated murder'.

The Birmingham Six and Guildford Four

Six Irishmen living in Britain were jailed for life for the 1974 Birmingham pub bombings, carried out by the IRA, in which twenty-one people died. The six claimed they were innocent. The scientific and confession evidence against them was finally shown to be unreliable and, sixteen years after their imprisonment, the six were released. In a similar case three Irishmen and an Englishwoman were jailed for pub bombings in Guildford, near London. In 1989 they were released when it was discovered that the evidence against them had been falsified by police.

The Royal Ulster Constabulary is the only permanently armed police force in the UK.

● The RUC and UDR

Two important parts of the British security forces in Ireland are recruited from inside Northern Ireland: the Royal Ulster Constabulary (RUC) and the Ulster Defence Regiment (UDR).

The RUC is the only fully armed police force in the UK. The UDR is a part of the British Army which was set up to defend Northern Ireland. Members of both forces are often singled out for attacks by the IRA.

Between 1969 and 1989, 263 members of the RUC have been killed and more than 8,000 injured. In the same period, the UDR suffered 181 deaths, the majority of them part-time soldiers who were killed while off-duty.

In his book on the RUC, the Northern Ireland journalist Chris Ryder writes:

> Interpol figures, published in the International Criminal Police Review in 1983, showed that Northern Ireland was the most dangerous place in the world to be a policeman. The risk factor was twice as high as in El Salvador, the second most dangerous . . . [in Northern Ireland] hatred of the police is all too often the primary purpose of the crime itself. (*The RUC: A Force Under Fire*, Chris Ryder.)

Casualties
Between 1969 and 1989 the security forces killed 178 civilians who had no connections to paramilitary groups. Source: Irish Information Partnership.

Members of the 'B Specials', the auxiliary police force in Northern Ireland, march to St Anne's Cathedral, Belfast, on 5 April 1970, for a service to mark the disbanding of the force. The Specials were dominated by Protestant members and were regarded as violently anti-Catholic.

British soldiers fire bullets at crowds in Belfast. These riot control weapons have killed seventeen people in Northern Ireland, many of them children.

The RUC is often accused of being anti-Catholic; only 10 per cent of its members are drawn from the Catholic community. The UDR has even fewer Catholic members. In 1988 only 3 per cent of its members were Catholics. In 1989, journalist Charles Townshend wrote:

> The UDR has never fulfilled its original task of becoming a bi-communal force [recruited from both Catholic and Protestant communities], and is regarded more or less as the old RUC B Specials who, after a faintly promising start in 1920, had degenerated into a sort of Protestant militia. (*The Times*, 9 August 1989.)

● The laboratory

Many people in Northern Ireland fear their homeland has become a testing ground, or 'laboratory' for the British security and intelligence services to try out new weapons and techniques. The methods used by the security forces to combat terrorism are often called into question.

In 1982 a special RUC squad shot dead five unarmed men and a seventeen-year-old youth, all Catholics. Some of the men were terrorist suspects. An English police officer, John Stalker, was sent by the government to investigate the 'shoot-to-kill' incidents. But in 1986 he was removed from the investigation.

> I believe, as do many members of the public, that I was hurriedly removed because I was on the threshold of causing a major police scandal and political row that would have resulted in several resignations and general mayhem. (*Stalker*, John Stalker.)

Security methods used in Northern Ireland:

- Internment (the jailing of suspects without a court hearing);
- Courts where there is no jury, only a judge who passes both verdict and sentence;
- Suspects have no right to remain silent;
- Use of high-technology surveillance and listening equipment;
- Use of plastic bullets and other riot control weapons. (Plastic and rubber bullets have killed seventeen people in Northern Ireland, nine were aged eighteen or under and two were only ten years old);
- Use of informers: in 1990 a man who informed on the IRA was reportedly paid £50,000 by the RUC for information supplied.

Some commentators argue that tactics used by British security forces in Northern Ireland have had a knock-on effect in Britain. Among the critics is Paul Foot, a left-wing British journalist who believes British security forces and British government should leave Northern Ireland:

> The chief effect [of the conflict in Northern Ireland] on us is the drain on our civil liberties. Bit by bit, the machinery of repression which the British government has constructed ... spreads its dark shadows over Britain. The Prevention of Terrorism Act allowed any citizen to be held without charge, trial or explanation for seven days. From 1974–1987, 6,430 people in Great Britain were detained in custody under the Act; 5,586 of these (87 per cent) were released without charge. From 1977–1986, 468,903 people were stopped and held for a while under the Act. In 1986 alone, 59,481 people were stopped ... This amounts to a vast infringement on the most fundamental liberties of thousands of citizens. (*Ireland: Why Britain Must Get Out*, Paul Foot.)

A Republican press conference in 1972. The man on the left of the picture is Martin McGuinness who is today a leading member of Sinn Fein, the political wing of the IRA. His voice was banned from radio and television in Britain and Ireland in 1988.

Media ban

In October 1988, the British government banned all television and radio companies from broadcasting interviews with named groups in Northern Ireland, including Sinn Fein and the UDA. The then British Prime Minister, Margaret Thatcher said of the ban: 'To beat off your enemy in a war you have to suspend some of your civil liberties for a time.' (*The Times*, 26 October 1988.)

Terrorists or freedom fighters?

A mural on the Falls Road, a nationalist area of Belfast, links the IRA's fight with the struggle of the Palestine Liberation Organization in the Middle East.

The history of Ireland is marred by violence, both in the shape of armed rebellion against British rule and conflict between the different traditions on the island. The violence which has raged in Northern Ireland since 1969 is seen as a continuation of that history by many of those who participate in and suffer from it.

● The IRA

The Irish Republican Army (IRA) is the most prominent, illegal paramilitary group involved in the Northern Ireland conflict. Also known as the Provisional IRA, following a split with the now defunct Official IRA in late 1969, the organization has a legal political wing called Sinn Fein (which means 'Ourselves Alone'). Other nationalist paramilitaries, such as the Irish National Liberation Army (INLA) have often been breakaway groups from the IRA.

The IRA is a force which has caused more death and destruction than the other paramilitaries. Of the 876 members of the security forces killed between 1969 and 1989, nationalist

> **The death toll**
> By the end of 1989 2,786 people in Northern Ireland had been killed in the course of the 'Troubles' out of a population of 1.6 million. The proportional number of casualties for Britain would be almost 100,000.

27

The office of Sinn Fein in Andersonstown, Belfast. The Christmas tree is covered with tags bearing the names of Republican 'prisoners of war'.

Punishment shootings

The paramilitaries virtually control some areas of Northern Ireland. These are areas where the police rarely patrol because they fear attack. The paramilitaries term crime in their areas 'anti-social behaviour' and they deal with it in a brutal way. They punish offenders by beating them, dropping concrete blocks on them, shooting them in the kneecaps or banishing them from Northern Ireland. The ultimate punishment is death.

---

paramilitaries, mainly the IRA, killed 847. Many of its own members or 'volunteers', who see themselves as dedicated soldiers, have died on what the IRA calls 'active service'. The IRA believes it has the right to wage war against Britain. Its secret manual, the *Green Book*, outlines its philosophy and ideology:

> The Irish Republican Army, as the legal representatives of the Irish people, are morally justified in carrying out a campaign of resistance against foreign occupation forces and domestic collaborators. (Quoted in *The IRA*, Tim Pat Coogan.)

But many people feel that the IRA's violent campaign is not morally justifiable. The IRA has been responsible for killing people simply because they are Protestant. It has also made what it calls 'mistakes' when it has missed its stated targets and killed innocent civilians. Nationalist paramilitaries were responsible for 574 civilian deaths between 1969 and 1989. In May 1990 the IRA shot dead two Australians holidaying in Holland having mistaken them for off-duty British soldiers. On Remembrance Sunday 1987, eleven civilians died when an IRA bomb exploded at a ceremony in Enniskillen, County Fermanagh. The IRA expressed 'deep regret' claiming that the bomb had gone off prematurely. The killings provoked disgust across the world and shamed many Republican supporters.

The membership of the IRA is drawn mainly from the Catholic community living in Northern Ireland. Many come from families with a Republican tradition. Patrick Bishop and Eamonn Mallie write, in the most recent authoritative account of the IRA:

> About 80 per cent of the current membership have fathers, uncles or brothers in the movement. Republicanism is a hereditary tradition and certain families exert a dominating influence on its history. Gerry Adams, the Sinn Fein president and pre-eminent figure among the small group that directs the Republican movement, has three brothers who are, or have been, in the organization, including one who until recently was head of the Belfast organization. As time has gone on, and the number of those who have experienced the death, wounding or imprisonment of a member of the family has multiplied, the potential recruiting base of the IRA has expanded correspondingly. (*The Provisional IRA*, Patrick Bishop and Eamonn Mallie.)

The IRA has proved itself to be durable and versatile. Its attacks have not been limited to Ireland. It has attacked the British military and government in Britain and Europe. Its attacks in Britain attract huge publicity and keep the IRA campaign of violence at the top of the political agenda when Ireland is being discussed. In October 1984 an IRA bomb wrecked the Grand Hotel, Brighton, where the leadership of the governing Conservative Party was staying during its annual conference. The Prime Minister, Margaret Thatcher, narrowly escaped, but several senior Conservative politicians were seriously injured and one was killed. In July 1990 an IRA car bomb killed Ian Gow, a Conservative MP, outside his south of England home. Mr Gow was a close personal friend of Margaret Thatcher.

> It is necessary, especially in a guerilla campaign, to attack the enemy on ground which you choose. To surprise the enemy, give them no rest, continually pressurize them, and, of course, hit them where it hurts … We can say that we intend to sap the British will to remain in our country and we have the ability to do so. We will fight the British on as many fronts as is logistically possible. (IRA spokesperson quoted in *Republican News*, June 1990.)

Above *Gerry Adams, leader of Sinn Fein and elected MP for West Belfast in 1983.*

Below *Brighton, October 1984, after an IRA bomb attack on the Grand Hotel, where leaders of the British government were staying.*

Masked and uniformed IRA 'volunteers' carry the coffin of Bobby Sands, the IRA man who was the first of ten Republicans to die in the Maze prison in 1981. He was on hunger strike, demanding to be given political prisoner status.

Hunger strikers

In April 1981 Bobby Sands, an IRA man serving a jail sentence in the Maze prison, was elected as MP for the Northern Ireland constituency of Fermanagh and South Tyrone. Sands was on hunger strike at the time, refusing food as part of a protest by Republican prisoners against their categorization in prison as criminals. The prisoners were demanding the status of political prisoners. They said they committed the offences they were jailed for because of the political situation in Ireland. Many graffiti writers wrote on walls:
I'll wear no convict's uniform
Nor meekly serve my time
That England might
Brand Ireland's fight
800 years of crime.
   Bobby Sands died on his sixty-sixth day without food. Nine other men were to fast to death before the protest ended. Today Republican and Loyalist prisoners are held separate from each other, operate military command structures in their blocks and hold political meetings.

British ministers and Army officers have admitted that the nature of the IRA makes it difficult to defeat. In a famous statement in 1971, British Home Secretary Reginald Maudling said, at the end of a visit to Northern Ireland:

> I don't think one can speak of defeating the IRA, of eliminating them completely, but it is the design of the security forces to reduce their level of violence to something like an acceptable level. (Quoted in *Phrases make History Here,* Conor O'Clery.)

● The Loyalist paramilitaries

There are two main paramilitary groups who describe themselves as Loyalist. They aim to prevent a united Ireland. The largest group is the Ulster Defence Association (UDA), which is still a legal organization but has a military wing, the Ulster Freedom Fighters (UFF), which is illegal. The other is the Ulster Volunteer Force (UVF), which is named after the group set up in 1912 when the British government seemed prepared to repeal the Act of Union and give Ireland independence.

Many Protestants fear that the IRA is waging a war directly against them – especially when it attacks the mainly Protestant members of the RUC and the UDR. The language of the Protestant paramilitaries reveals a siege mentality. They do not trust the British government to protect them and fear they are surrounded by hostile forces. A 1973 UDA statement revealed Loyalist extremists' fears, in the wake of talks between nationalist and Unionist parties about a power-sharing government for Northern Ireland:

> We are betrayed, maligned and our families live in constant fear and misery. We are a nuisance to our so-called allies and have no friends anywhere. Once more in the history of our people, we have our backs to the wall, facing extinction by one way or another. This is the moment to beware, for Ulstermen in this position fight mercilessly till they or their enemies are dead. (Quoted in *Northern Ireland: the International Perspective,* Adrian Guelke.)

On occasions the Loyalist paramilitaries have drawn parallels between what they see as their besieged situation and the position of white South Africans, under pressure to grant black majority rule, and Israel, surrounded by unfriendly Arab states. A 1970s UFF press release claimed:

> We have more in common with the state of Israel . . . Those brave people fought and won their battle for survival. We intend to win ours. And like the Jewish people, each time an act of aggression is committed against our people, we shall retaliate in a way that only the animals in the IRA can understand. (Quoted in *Northern Ireland: the International Perspective,* Adrian Guelke.)

But often their retaliation has been simply anti-Catholic rather than targeted on the IRA. Between 1969 and 1989, Loyalist groups killed twenty-one nationalist paramilitaries and 632 civilians, 506 of whom were Catholics.

Members of the Protestant paramilitary Ulster Defence Association (UDA) march through Belfast wearing caps and dark glasses to disguise their identity. The UDA is a legal organization but it has an offshoot called the Ulster Freedom Fighters which is banned.

Demonstrators in New York, USA, burn the Union Flag outside the British Consulate in 1981 during the hunger strike at the Maze prison. The Republican movement in Northern Ireland has many supporters in the USA, some of whom have supplied money and weapons.

Shankhill butchers

Between November 1975 and February 1977 a Loyalist murder gang known as the Shankhill Butchers carried out a series of hideous murders of Catholics in Belfast. The victims were apparently targeted simply because they were Catholic. As many as nineteen people may have been killed by the gang. Some were battered to death, others were slowly strangled in a home-made torture chamber. The gang earned its name by finishing off its victims with meat cleavers or axes. In 1979 eight members of the gang were given a total of forty-two life sentences. One man who received an eight-year sentence for his involvement with the gang had been a member of the Ulster Defence Regiment, part of the security forces, at the time of the murders.

● International support

The IRA's most important international support, in the shape of weapons and money, has come from two main sources overseas. For generations, Irish people have emigrated to the USA. In the 1980 US Census 43.7 million people (19 per cent of the population) defined themselves as Irish. Many of those people support the ideas of Irish nationalism. Through organizations like Noraid they contribute money to help Republican causes and organizations in Ireland. One of its former leaders, Michael Flannery, proudly boasts of his gun-running activities.

> He confirmed that Noraid, under his leadership, had never been involved in gun-running to the IRA. However, he said that he personally, while chairman of Noraid, had led a successful gun-running unit from 1970 to 1981. Indeed he had been doing it on and off for 'about 25 years.' . . . 'We sent them [guns] as agricultural implements and so forth . . . We sent them through reputable companies in Ireland . . . It was a very secretive and solid bit of work. We had people in the companies and on the docks, so they never discovered anything.' ('Fast Talkers and Fenians,' Peter Lennon, the *Guardian*, 17 July 1990.)

A legal clampdown on the activities of American gun-runners forced the IRA to turn to other sources of supply. The most prominent supplier in recent years, according to intelligence sources, has been the Libyan government led by Colonel Gadaffi. Libya is said to have sent massive shiploads of arms to Ireland, including a large quantity of the plastic explosive Semtex, which is now a major part of the IRA's armoury. As long ago as June 1972, during a speech in Tripoli, the Libyan leader stated:

> We support the Irish revolutionaries who are fighting Britain ... we have strong ties with the revolutionaries to whom we have supplied arms. (Quoted in *Phrases Make History Here*, Conor O'Clery.)

Loyalist groups have received financial support from sympathetic emigrant groups across the world, most notably in Canada and Scotland. Some Protestant paramilitaries have claimed to have attended training camps in Israel and South Africa.

In April 1989, three members of the Loyalist group Ulster Resistance (which Ian Paisley's Democratic Unionist Party helped to launch) and a South African diplomat were arrested in Paris. An American arms dealer was also present. The meeting had been arranged to swap South African arms for missile parts being made for the British military which had been stolen from a factory in Belfast.

Arms dumps stored by the paramilitaries are often uncovered by the security forces in Northern Ireland. In this case in 1988 the arms belonged to Loyalist groups and included thirty light sub-machine guns.

A youth in Derry/Londonderry siphons petrol from a Royal Mail van to use in the making of petrol bombs, the rioter's favourite weapon.

● Racketeering

Paramilitaries from both sides are widely believed to have been involved in protection and extortion rackets within Northern Ireland in order to gain money. They demand money from building contractors and the owners of public houses and drinking clubs.

In March 1990 it emerged that Loyalist paramilitaries may have stolen £500,000 of government money by tampering with contracts for maintenance and building work on an Army base in Ballykelly, County Derry. In the same month the Bank of Ireland said it had received a £2 million extortion demand, reportedly from the IRA.

In Irish novelist Brian Moore's *Lies of Silence* Moira Dillon loses her temper with IRA gunmen who are holding her hostage. Her feelings reflect a widely held sentiment in Northern Ireland:

> You're just a bunch of crooks, IRA or UDA, Protestants or Catholics, you're all in the same business. Racketeers the bunch of you. There isn't a building site in this city or a pub that you or the UDA don't hold up for protection money. Protection money! You've made this place into a bloody shambles and if it was handed over to your crowd tomorrow, lock, stock and barrel, you wouldn't have the first notion of what to do with it . . . You're not fighting for anybody's freedom. Not mine, not the people of Northern Ireland's, not anybody's. The only thing you're doing is making people hate each other worse than ever. Maybe that's what you want isn't it? Because if the Catholics stopped hating the Prods [Protestants], where would the IRA be? (*Lies of Silence*, Brian Moore.)

1 Do you think any group in Northern Ireland has the right to use violence in pursuit of its aims?

2 What do you think the Protestant paramilitary groups are defending? What do you think the Catholic paramilitary groups are attacking?

3 Do you think members of paramilitary groups who are arrested should be treated as ordinary criminals, or should their political motives entitle them to different treatment as political prisoners?

6

So what's it like to live in Northern Ireland?

● **A special place**

> For most of the people in Northern Ireland the TV pictures and the news reports of killings and bombings and riots are almost as distant in psychological [mental] terms as they are for people in Britain. Almost everyone in Northern Ireland goes about his or her business in exactly the same way as people in Britain and the rest of Ireland. In purely statistical terms the risk of being caught up in terrorist or sectarian violence is really quite low. The risk of death or serious injury as a result of the 'troubles' is now less than half the risk of being killed or injured in a traffic accident. It is far more dangerous to live in New York or Detroit or many other large American cities than it is to live in Belfast. (*Ireland: A Positive Proposal,* Kevin Boyle and Tom Hadden.)

It is more common for Northern Irish people to fall in love, get married and have children than it is for them to try to hurt each other. Northern Irish children grow up, look for a job and a place to live, make friends, go on holiday. There are cities, towns and villages, beautiful countryside with rivers, mountains, loughs and a spectacular coastline.

The Divis flats in Belfast, a complex of sprawling high-rise blocks which were unpopular among residents.

The Cornmarket, a pedestrianized area of Belfast City centre, popular as a meeting place and a shopping precinct.

● Homes

Most people in Northern Ireland live in rented homes. Of the people living in government housing in 1987, two in every three could not afford to pay the rent. Families are larger than the UK average size and in some cases there is severe overcrowding. In 1980, the British social affairs journalist Polly Toynbee reported:

> Mrs Rooney has lived in the flats for six years with her five children, aged 11 to 24, in two bedrooms. Her husband is on night work so the girls sleep with their mother, and the boys in the other room. At weekends when their father is home, the girls sleep on the sitting-room floor. (Polly Toynbee, from a week of special features in the *Guardian,* 18–23 February 1980.)

In 1987, a survey of all homes in Northern Ireland found that 28.7 per cent were in a poor state of repair, or unfit to live in. It also found that the people living in unfit buildings could not afford to pay for the repairs themselves. Polly Toynbee wrote of the Divis Estate, a collection of ugly tower block flats, in West Belfast:

> The troubles have contributed to the plight of the estate but wherever it had been thrown up, it would have sunk under its own architectural and design faults, the cheapness of the materials used, the lack of repairs and amenities. (Polly Toynbee, from a week of special features in the *Guardian,* 18–23 February 1980.)

● The economy

Northern Ireland is not a rich place. Its economy faces a number of geographical problems. It is in a remote location. It lacks a supply of industrial raw materials; essential basics like fuel and metals must be imported before anything can be manufactured there. Agriculture is important to the Northern Ireland economy. The land is fertile and most of it is farmed. Cattle and dairy products make up the largest part of production. Potatoes are the region's biggest crop.

Since the world recession of the late 1970s the Northern Irish economy has shifted to service industries. Forty per cent of employment is now in public sector services like education, health and administration. On average, people remain 25 per cent worse off than residents in the rest of the UK.

Unemployment is high in Northern Ireland. Some people have never had a job since leaving school, many more find work only for a short time. Many young people choose to emigrate; 8,000 people left Northern Ireland in 1988 to live elsewhere. Almost half the unemployed people of Northern Ireland live in Belfast. But Belfast is still the best place to find work. The western town of Strabane, on the border with Donegal, has long had the highest unemployment rate. It has 23 per cent unemployment; more than 60 per cent of the unemployed there had been out of work for over a year in 1989. The poor performance of the economy means many people are dependent on state benefits. Figures quoted in one mid-1980s survey have not altered much:

> In 1983 22 per cent of Northern Ireland's total population was wholly or partly supported by state benefits, compared with 13 per cent in Britain in 1982. (*On The Edge: a study of poverty and long term unemployment in Northern Ireland*, Eileen Evason.)

Figures released in February 1990 show that identifiable public spending per head for the four countries of the UK were as follows: Northern Ireland, £3,626; Scotland, £2,805; Wales, £2,489; England, £2,161. The average for the UK was £2,275.

Population

In 1988 the population of Northern Ireland was 1,578,100: 803,600 females and 774,500 males. Belfast was the biggest city with a population of 299,600. Derry/Londonderry, the second city, had a population of 98,700. Of the 8.2 per cent of the population who are over seventy, two-thirds are women. In 1988 27,767 babies were born in Northern Ireland (there were more boys than girls), while 15,813 people died. The population is expected to grow at 1 per cent per year until the early twenty-first century.

● The crack

There is no easy translation of what the Irish mean by 'the crack'. They ask each other 'What's the crack?', meaning 'How are things?' 'What's going on?' 'Any news?' They say 'The crack was great,' when recalling laughter and jokes, drinking and dancing, music and song. People in Northern Ireland do not talk about having a good time, they talk about 'the crack'.

The use of a word like 'crack' is typical of the specialness Northern Ireland enjoys. Despite poor housing conditions, overcrowding and low incomes, the visitor receives a warm welcome in Catholic and Protestant homes.

> Their houses were kept like 'little palaces' – extremely clean and tidy – and the pictures of the Royal Family on the walls were always carefully dusted. They called the [church] minister . . . 'Frosty' because he was not as warm and informal as they were. (*Loyal to King Billy: A Portrait of the Ulster Protestants*, Robert G Crawford.)

Traditional musicians entertain drinkers in a Belfast club.

> In the tiny snug living rooms, each with turf or coal fire and Sacred Heart on the wall, the sofas and chairs were constantly filled with people and more on the floor, together often with a horrible old dog; the television was on in the corner but no one was looking; there was too much to say, and the humanity of the atmosphere was as warming to some chilly part of the soul as the fire to the sodden feet. (*The Crack: A Belfast Year*, Sally Belfrage.)

Nearly 1 million people visit Northern Ireland each year. Only 150,000 are tourists. Many more are emigrants who come home to visit families. The most popular holiday destinations are Belfast and the beaches of Portrush and Portstewart on the north coast.

Each year Belfast hosts a festival which attracts international talent. Because the city is more famous as a bomb site than a place of entertainment, artists and performers from abroad are uncertain about appearing in one of the world's 'trouble spots'. But as the arts critic Michael Billington discovered:

> Once they've savoured Belfast's hospitality and insatiable hunger for visitors, they willingly return. (From a week of special features in the *Guardian*, 18–23 February 1980.)

Salmon fishermen at Carrick-a-rede on the Antrim coast. The rugged, beautiful coastline attracts visitors from overseas and is very popular with the people of Northern Ireland.

Irish writers are famed the world over. Northern Ireland's most famous living poet is Seamus Heaney. He is the elected Professor of Poetry at Oxford University. This is an extract from his poem 'Digging', which he wrote in 1966.

A man cutting turf in an Irish peat bog. In rural areas many families own parts of a peat bog from which they gather fuel for winter fires.

> *Between my finger and my thumb*
> *The squat pen rests; snug as a gun . . .*
>
> *My grandfather cut more turf in a day*
> *Than any other man on Toner's bog.*
> *Once I carried him milk in a bottle*
> *Corked sloppily with paper.*
> *He straightened up*
> *To drink it, then fell to right away*
> *Nicking and slicing neatly, heaving sods*
> *Over his shoulder, going down and down*
> *For the good turf. Digging.*
> *The cold smell of potato mould, the squelch and slap*
> *Of soggy peat, the curt cuts of an edge*
> *Through living roots awaken in my head.*
> *But I've no spade to follow men like them.*
>
> *Between my finger and my thumb*
> *The squat pen rests.*
> *I'll dig with it.*

(*New Selected Poems*, Seamus Heaney.)

As the Irish writer Polly Devlin says, it is a special place:

> Northern Ireland is for us neither one thing nor the other; in it we are neither English nor Irish. (*All Of Us There*, Polly Devlin.)

> 1 What do you think it would be like to live in Northern Ireland today?
>
> 2 What's your idea of 'good crack'?

7

Solutions

> One of the most striking things about the Irish problem is that there are so many solutions. Literally hundreds of possible settlements have been proposed. (*Ireland: A Positive Proposal*, Kevin Boyle and Tom Hadden.)

● A united Ireland

A united Ireland has been put forward by many as the solution to the Northern Ireland problem.

> The idea of Ireland as a natural political unit that must ultimately be united in a single independent state is deeply imbedded in the nationalist and Republican traditions . . . Commitment to the ideal of unification is deeply rooted in the Republic, in the nationalist community in Northern Ireland and among Irish emigrants throughout the world. The only significant dispute has been whether the ideal can be achieved only by force . . . or whether it can be achieved peacefully and by consent. (Ireland: *A Positive Proposal*, Kevin Boyle and Tom Hadden.)

A Republican mural in West Belfast looks to the past to link the rebels of 1916 with the IRA of today. The word saoirse *means 'freedom'.*

The fundamental aim of the Republican movement is the achievement of a united Ireland. According to Gerry Adams the president of Sinn Fein:

> Republicans seek to force Britain to stop supporting the Irish minority – the unionists – and to concede the indivisible national rights of the Irish people as a whole . . . But all sensible people agree that the consent of Northern Protestants, like any other interest group, is desirable on the constitutional, financial and political arrangements needed to replace partition . . . We need them because a peaceful, just and united society in Ireland must include them. (*A Pathway to Peace,* Gerry Adams.)

Despite those words of compromise for Northern Ireland Protestants, the Republicans believe that armed force can be used to obtain Irish unity. Sinn Fein's deputy president Martin McGuinness says:

> I believe the armed struggle can be justified, even though I don't like it. I don't like the fact that Irish men and women have to resort to force of arms. But I believe that strategy holds out the hope of a British Government at some time in the future being so embarrassed and so ridiculed throughout the world by their inability to resolve a problem – which should be more resolvable than the problems that are now being resolved in Eastern Europe . . . – that they have to take positive radical action. (Quoted in the Dublin magazine *Hot Press* 22 March 1990.)

Some nationalists believe a united Ireland can be achieved without force and with the consent of the Northern Protestants. The clearest statement of a peacefully united Ireland has come from the New Ireland Forum, a conference involving the Republic of Ireland's main political parties and the moderate nationalist party, the SDLP, from Northern Ireland. The Final Report of the Forum in May 1984 stated that:

> . . . a united Ireland in the form of a sovereign independent Irish state to be achieved peacefully and by consent . . . [is] the best and most durable basis for peace and stability . . . [a single state] would embrace the whole island of Ireland governed as a single unit under one government and one parliament elected by all the people of the island. (*Final Report,* New Ireland Forum.)

Members of the British left-wing organization, the Irish Freedom Movement, march through London to call for the withdrawal of British troops from Northern Ireland.

This approach to a united Ireland was welcomed by the British Labour Party, which has a policy on Ireland of 'unity by consent'. The New Ireland Forum report also offered two other ways in which Ireland could be united: as a federal state with four regional governments, one in each of the provinces of Ulster, Leinster, Munster and Connaught; or with Northern Ireland coming under the 'joint authority' of the British and Irish governments. However, a united Ireland is largely an unacceptable option for Northern Ireland's Protestants.

> A united Ireland is far and away the most popular solution outside of Northern Ireland, but such is the resistance to this option within Northern Ireland from the majority, that its imposition would require the military subjugation of the Protestant community. (*Northern Ireland: the International Perspective*, Adrian Guelke.)

● A new Northern Ireland

Unionist thought on a solution to the Northern Ireland problem has revolved around three basic ideas:
1) a new regional government for Northern Ireland;
2) the full integration of the North into the UK;
3) the declaration of an independent Northern Ireland.

Political groups in Northern Ireland use every opportunity to get their message across. Mural-painting has become an established medium for propaganda.

Loyalists waving Union and Ulster flags in protests against the Anglo-Irish Agreement. The accord gave the Irish government some say in how Northern Ireland was ruled. Loyalists saw it as a 'sell out' and their slogan was 'Ulster Says No.'

The Assembly

In 1982 elections were held for the Northern Ireland Assembly, another British attempt to solve the problem. From the beginning, nationalist politicians in the SDLP and Sinn Fein refused to take their seats in the Assembly. Only the unionists and the non-sectarian Alliance Party took their seats. The Assembly was dissolved in 1986 after it had become little more than a forum for unionist protest against the Anglo-Irish Agreement.

● A new regional government

Many unionist politicians favour the restoration of an elected government for Northern Ireland, similar to the one that was abolished in 1972. They distrust direct rule from London and believe it is undemocratic. In 1984, the Ulster Unionist Party policy paper *The Way Forward* stated:

> In only one part of the United Kingdom, namely Northern Ireland, are major services [ie health, education, social security, police etc] subject to no real democratic control. In Northern Ireland alone do employers and professional staff, who would normally take their instructions directly from elected representatives, take their orders from civil servants . . .
> (Quoted in *Unfinished Business,* Liam de Paor.)

But a new locally elected government may not be acceptable to the nationalist population in Northern Ireland. They fear it would be unionist-controlled, like the government which from 1921 to 1972 treated them as second-class citizens.

Many Catholics might accept a regional government in which their representatives were allowed to share power. British attempts to bring the Northern Ireland parties together have been based on creating a power-sharing regime. So far, only a small minority of unionists have come out in favour of power-sharing.

Schoolchildren in a nationalist area of Belfast find a high vantage point in 1972 to watch the passing of a Republican parade commemorating the 1916 rising.

1 What do you think is the best solution to the problems of Northern Ireland?

2 Do you think that both Protestants and Catholics would be happy with your solution? How do you think people in Britain, the Republic of Ireland and other countries might react?

● Integration

As we have seen, Northern Ireland is very different from Britain. Many of the laws governing Northern Ireland (from divorce and abortion to security measures) are very different from laws in the rest of the UK. Most of Britain's political parties do not contest elections in Northern Ireland. Some unionists believe the best way to secure the link with Britain is to absorb Northern Ireland fully into the UK and allow Northern Ireland voters to choose between the British parties who govern them.

> It would allow the citizens of Ulster the chance to choose between the programmes held out to them by nationalist and Unionist parties and the alternatives of Left, Right and Centre, which determine their material welfare . . . Catholics have a right to equal opportunities within Northern Ireland . . . and both Ulster Catholics and Protestants have a right to equality of opportunity within the United Kingdom. (*Under Siege,* Arthur Aughey.)

But integration takes no account of the Irish identity felt by so many in Northern Ireland and is likely to be opposed strongly by the nationalist population. Successive British governments have shown no inclination to integrate the complications of Northern Ireland into the rest of the UK.

● Independence

The New Ulster Political Research Group, an offshoot of the UDA, proposed an independent Northern Ireland in 1979 as:

> . . . the only proposal which does not have a victor and a loser. It will encourage the development of a common identity between all of our people, regardless of religion. We offer through our proposal, first class Ulster citizenship to all of our people, because, like it or not, the Protestant of Northern Ireland is looked upon as a second class British citizen in Britain and the Roman Catholic of Northern Ireland as a second class Irish citizen in the South. (Quoted in *Northern Ireland: the International Perspective,* Adrian Guelke.)

But independence has little support among either nationalists or unionists. It is unlikely that an independent Northern Ireland would be economically strong enough to survive on its own. Many unionists have contemplated independence as a 'last resort' option should Britain decide to leave Ireland.

These unionists envisage a repartition of Northern Ireland into a smaller area with a strong Protestant majority. In the aftermath of the Anglo-Irish Agreement, when many Protestants feared Britain was preparing to withdraw, Alan Wright, leader of the Ulster Clubs organization, said:

> Left on their own after a British pull-out, Loyalists would build a Berlin-type wall from Londonderry to Newry, with four border crossings and a 100-yard [31m] strip mined and patrolled 24 hours a day. There would be conscription for the 18 to 21-year-olds whose sole duty would be to combat militant nationalism. (Quoted in *Phrases Make History Here*, Conor O'Clery.)

Some have argued that whatever solution is put forward, it will only succeed if the grievances that fuel the violence are themselves addressed. Historian Liam de Paor puts it this way:

> Terrorism must indeed be defeated. But not by shooting suspects dead at checkpoints, by SAS assassinations, by beatings in police cells, by midnight searches of working-class homes, by the testimony of perjurers in Diplock courts [courts with no jury] presided over by deeply prejudiced judges. Rather it must be defeated by depriving terrorists of their support, which means making life tolerable for all in Northern Ireland. (*Unfinished Business*, Liam de Paor.)

Mairead Corrigan (second from left) and Betty Williams (third from left) led the Women's Peace Movement which attracted huge support in Northern Ireland in 1976. Their campaign lost support when it became almost solely an anti-IRA movement and did not criticize the violence of the security forces. Many ordinary people became disillusioned with the 'Peace People' when the leaders started jetting around the world and receiving huge amounts of money in donations. The movement petered out. There has been no serious large-scale peace campaign since.

Glossary

Catholic A member of the Roman Catholic Church.

Extortion To get hold of someone's money by intimidating him or her.

Federal Relating to a form of government in which power is divided between one central and several regional governments.

Free State The name given to the twenty-six-county state in Southern Ireland in 1921 when limited independence from Britain was achieved.

Interpol (International Criminal Police Organization) An association of over 100 national police forces, devoted chiefly to fighting international crime.

IRA (Irish Republican Army) The foremost nationalist paramilitary organization, which says it is fighting a war against Britain to achieve a united, independent Irish Republic. It split in 1969 into two factions: the Official IRA, which favoured political action and the Provisional IRA, which followed the traditional policy of using force to achieve Irish Unity. The Official IRA is now defunct, so the Provisional IRA tends to be known simply as the IRA.

Mass The celebration of the Eucharist (in the Roman Catholic Church and certain Protestant Churches).

Nationalist A person who aspires to the political aim of a united Ireland. Hardline nationalists are usually called Republicans. Also used in reference to those people in Northern Ireland who see themselves as Irish rather than British.

Northern Ireland The British-controlled state established in 1921. Made up of the six north-eastern counties of Ireland.

Northern Ireland Office The department of the British government responsible for Northern Ireland affairs.

Orange Order A men-only, Protestant-only organization established in 1795 to celebrate the victories of William of Orange, who secured the Protestant succession to the English throne at the Battle of the Boyne in 1690.

Paramilitary A word used to denote an organization with a military structure, and which uses military techniques, but is not a part of the official security forces.

Partition The division of Ireland into two states as outlined by the British parliament in the 1920 Government of Ireland Act.

Protestant A member of one of the Western Christian Churches that are separated from the Roman Catholic Church.

Republic of Ireland The twenty-six-county Southern Irish state as it is known today.

RUC (Royal Ulster Constabulary) The police force of Northern Ireland and the only fully armed police force in the UK.

Sectarianism Adherence to a particular sect, faction or doctrine and intolerance of other groups; in Northern Ireland violence between Protestants and Catholics is described as sectarian.

Security forces The general term applied to British government forces in Northern Ireland: the British Army, RUC and UDR.

Troubles The name given to the current spate of fighting in Ireland which began in 1969.

UDA (Ulster Defence Association) The largest of the Loyalist paramilitary groups in Northern Ireland.

UDR (Ulster Defence Regiment) A part of the British Army which is recruited and serves only in Northern Ireland. Many of its members serve on a part-time basis.

UK (United Kingdom of Great Britain and Northern Ireland) Formed in 1922 after the Partition of Ireland. Great Britain includes England, Wales and Scotland. Before 1922 it was the United Kingdom of Great Britain and Ireland.

Unionist A person who supports the continuation of the Union – the formal political link between Ireland and Britain. Hardline unionists are often called Loyalists. The term is often applied to those people in Northern Ireland who see themselves as British rather than Irish.

Further information

Statistics and information on the violence in Northern Ireland, including the examples used in this book are available from:

The Irish Information Partnership, PO Box 1894, London NW1 0SQ

Other information is available from:

Information on Ireland, PO Box 958, London W14 0JF

Sinn Fein Foreign Affairs Bureau, 51/55 Falls Road, Belfast BT12

The Democratic Unionist Party, 296 Albert Bridge Road, Belfast BT5 4GX

The Friends of the Union, 2 Swan Walk, London SW3 4JJ

The Irish Embassy, 16 Grosvenor Place, London SW1 7HH

The Northern Ireland Office Information Service, Stormont Castle, Belfast BT4 3ST

The Social Democratic and Labour Party, 24 Mount Charles, Belfast BT7 1NZ

Ulster Unionist Information Institute, 3 Glengall Street, Belfast BT12 5AE

In Canada:

Irish United Information Service, PO Box 561, Pickering, Ontario L1V 2RY

The British High Commission, 80 Elgin Street, Ottawa K1P 5K7

Further reading

A History of Northern Ireland, Patrick Buckland (Gill and Macmillan, 1981)

Ireland for Beginners, P Evans and E Polloch (Writers and Readers, 1983) (Pro-Republican cartoon history.)

Northern Ireland: A Political Directory, WD Flackes and Sydney Elliott (Blackstaff Press, 1989)

Northern Ireland: Questions of Nuance, Padraig O'Malley (Blackstaff Press, 1990)

Northern Ireland Soldiers Talking, Max Arthur (Sidgwick and Jackson, 1987)

Only the Rivers Run Free, Fairweather, McDonagh, McFadyean (Pluto, 1983)

Phrases Make History Here, Conor O'Clery (O'Brien Press, 1986)

The Crack, A Belfast Year, Sally Belfrage (Andre Deutsch, 1987)

The Ould Orange Flute, H McDonnell (Blackstaff Press, 1983)

The Provisional IRA, Patrick Bishop and Eamonn Mallie (Corgi, 1988)

The Uncivil Wars: Ireland Today, Padraig O'Malley (Blackstaff Press, 1983)

War and an Irish Town, Eamonn McCann (Pluto, 1980). (A highly readable account of the beginning of the 'Troubles' in Derry/Londonderry.)

Picture acknowledgements

The map on page 9 is by Peter Bull.

The Publisher would like to thank the following for providing photographs for use as illustrations in this book: *Belfast Telegraph* 7, 13, 18, 24, 26; E T Archive 6, 10 (Ulster Museum), 15 (National Library of Ireland); Eye Ubiquitous 14 (Trisha Rafferty), 27 (Paul Seheult), 28 (Paul Seheult), 36 (Steven Rafferty), 42; *Living Marxism* 34 (Joe Boatman), 41 (Joe Boatman); Network *cover* (Homer Sykes), 11 (John Sturrock), 16 (John Sturrock), 20, 23 (Barry Lewis), 29 bottom (Mike Abrahams), 37 (Mike Abrahams), 40 (Barry Lewis), 45 (Homer Sykes); Northern Ireland Tourist Board 38; Popperfoto 12, 22, 30, 35 (Richard Butchins); Topham 4, 5, 8, 17, 19, 21, 25, 29 top, 31, 32, 33, 39, 43, 44.

Index

Numbers in **bold** refer to pictures as well as text.